YOUR KNOWLEDGE HAS VALUE

AF153557

- We will publish your bachelor's and master's thesis, essays and papers

- Your own eBook and book - sold worldwide in all relevant shops

- Earn money with each sale

Upload your text at www.GRIN.com and publish for free

The Global Financial Crisis of 2008

A Critical Analysis of the Failures and Weaknesses in the Corporate Governance Arrangements

Brian Khisa

Bibliographic information published by the German National Library:

The German National Library lists this publication in the National Bibliography; detailed bibliographic data are available on the Internet at http://dnb.dnb.de.

ISBN: 9783346973382
This book is also available as an ebook.

© GRIN Publishing GmbH
Trappentreustraße 1
80339 München

Print and binding: Books on Demand GmbH, Norderstedt, Germany
Printed on acid-free paper from responsible sources.

The present work has been carefully prepared. Nevertheless, authors and publishers do not incur liability for the correctness of information, notes, links and advice as well as any printing errors.

GRIN web shop: https://www.grin.com/document/1420489

THE GLOBAL FINANCIAL CRISIS OF 2008

A CRITICAL ANALYSIS OF THE FAILURES AND WEAKNESSES IN THE CORPORATE GOVERNANCE ARRANGEMENTS

BRIAN KHISA SIMIYU

INTERNATIONAL CORPORATE GOVERNANCE

JUNE 12, 2023

CONTENTS

1.0   **INTRODUCTION** 2

2.0   **CORPORATE GOVERNANCE AND THE 2008 GLOBAL FINANCIAL CRISIS** 4

    2.1   DEFINITION OF CORPORATE GOVERNANCE 5

    2.2   THE ROLE OF CORPORATE GOVERNANCE 6

    2.3   THE 2008 GLOBAL FINANCIAL CRISIS 7

    2.4   CORPORATE GOVERNANCE BEFORE THE 2008 GLOBAL FINANCIAL CRISIS 8

       2.4.1   *Shareholder Value* 9

       2.4.2   *Risk Management* 9

       2.4.3   *Executive Remuneration* 9

       2.4.4   *Board Independence* 9

       2.4.5   *Regulatory Frameworks* 10

    2.5   FAILURES AND WEAKNESSES IN THE CORPORATE GOVERNANCE ARRANGEMENTS 10

3.0   **LIMITATIONS OF THE STUDY** 11

4.0   **A CRITICAL DISCUSSION OF GRANT KIRKPATRICK'S STATEMENT** 11

    4.1   MERITS OF GRANT KIRKPATRICK'S STATEMENT 12

       4.1.1   *Poor Risk Management* 12

       4.1.2   *Absence of Board Oversight* 12

       4.1.3   *Lack of Transparency and Accountability* 12

       4.1.4   *Executive Remuneration System* 13

    4.2   DEMERITS OF GRANT KIRKPATRICK'S STATEMENT 13

       4.2.1   *Failures in Regulation* 13

       4.2.2   *Shared Responsibility* 14

       4.2.3   *Broader Systemic Causes* 14

5.0   **CONCLUSION** 14

    BIBLIOGRAPHY 16

"The financial crisis can be to an important extent attributed to failures and weaknesses in corporate governance arrangements. When they were put to a test, corporate governance routines did not serve their purpose to safeguard against excessive risk taking..."

- **Grant Kirkpatrick, 'The Corporate Governance Lessons from the Financial Crisis' (2009) OECD 2**

Critically discuss this statement.

1.0 INTRODUCTION

A catastrophic global economic crisis that started in the United States and expanded rapidly to all other countries around the world was the "Global Financial Crisis of 2008." In terms of its scope and magnitude of effect, The Great Depression of the 1930's is largely regarded as having caused a more significant financial catastrophe than the one witnessed in the 2008 Global Financial Crisis.[1] It is noted that several issues, including shortcomings in corporate governance, might have led to the 2008 Global Financial Crisis. The 2008 Global Financial Crisis brought to light a number of supervision and accountability issues with financial institutions, which contributed to their collapse and the ensuing impacts on the rest of the world's economy from a corporate governance perspective.

Corporate Governance is the term used to describe the procedures and frameworks used to command, control, and run businesses. It includes all interactions among a company's management, board of directors, shareholders, and other stakeholders. By focusing on maximizing long-term shareholder value while taking into account the interests of other stakeholders, effective corporate governance ensures that businesses are governed responsibly

---

[1] Adrian Blundell-Wignall, Paul Atkinson and Se Hoon Lee, 'The current financial crisis: Causes and policy issues' (2009) 2008 OECD Journal: Financial market trends 1

and transparently. This was shown by Kirkpatrick,[2] Cheffins,[3] and Grosse[4] who ascribed the primary reasons for the 2008 Global Financial Crisis to inability of a company's management to protect the company from taking on too much risk and to provide effective board monitoring.

According to Grant Kirkpatrick's analysis of the impact of failures and weaknesses in corporate governance on the 2008 Global Financial Crisis,[5] it was concluded that the financial crisis can to a significant extent be attributed to failures and weaknesses in corporate governance arrangements that did not serve their purpose to safeguard against excessive risk taking in a number of financial services companies. Grant Kirkpatrick's remark emphasizes the major contribution that inadequacies and failures in corporate governance frameworks made to the 2008 Global Financial Crisis. It implies that corporate governance procedures fell short of their goal of protecting against excessive risk-taking.

Accordingly, this essay seeks to critically discuss the statement by evaluating the rationale behind the statement as a whole while taking into account the concurring and oppositional viewpoints regarding the statement. The essay discusses whether and to what extent corporate governance may be regarded as a significant contributing factor to the 2008 Global Financial Crisis through the lenses of risk management as a crucial component of Corporate Governance. In order to conclusively and objectively analyze the statement, the essay evaluates both the merits and demerits of Kirkpatrick's argument that "the financial crisis can be to an important extent attributed to failures and weaknesses in corporate governance arrangements."

---

[2] Grant Kirkpatrick, 'The corporate governance lessons from the financial crisis' (2009) 2009 OECD Journal: Financial market trends 61
[3] Brian R Cheffins, 'Did Corporate Governance" Fail" During the 2008 Stock Market Meltdown? The Case of the S&P 500' (2009) The Business Lawyer 1
[4] Robert E Grosse, 'The global financial crisis–a behavioral view' (2010) Available at SSRN 1537744
[5] Kirkpatrick, 'The corporate governance lessons from the financial crisis'

The essay begins by evaluating the key literature on Corporate Governance and the Global Financial Crisis of 2008. A definition of corporate governance and the role of corporate governance is highlighted to provide analytical context into the 2008 Global Financial Crisis and the failure and weaknesses in the corporate governance structures that led to the crisis. The merits and demerits of Grant Kirkpatrick's statement are then critically discussed in succinct detail. The essay ultimately concludes by concurring with Kirkpatrick's assertion that financial institutions did not follow corporate governance guidelines, which view risk management as an obvious oversight responsibility of the board of directors that would be satisfied by assessing the success of the company's risk strategies and making the necessary adjustments.

2.0 CORPORATE GOVERNANCE AND THE 2008 GLOBAL FINANCIAL CRISIS

The origins of the 2008 Global Financial Crisis have been the subject of several studies and analyses throughout the years.[6] Many academics have pointed to corporate governance as one of the primary causes of the crisis, with other aspects only simply playing a supporting role.[7] It has been argued severally that the failure of several financial institutions and the ensuing crisis were caused by several flaws in the corporate governance structure and procedures. It has also been observed that before and even during the crisis, many banks and financial firms did not pay enough attention to corporate governance.

---

[6] Thomas Clarke, 'Recurring crises in Anglo-American corporate governance' (2010) 29 Contributions to Political Economy 9; Mr Luc Laeven and others, *Lessons and policy implications from the global financial crisis* (International Monetary Fund 2010); William W Lang and Julapa A Jagtiani, 'The mortgage and financial crises: The role of credit risk management and corporate governance' (2010) 38 Atlantic Economic Journal 295; Hussein Tarraf, 'Literature review on corporate governance and the recent financial crisis' (2010) Available at SSRN 1731044

[7] Kirkpatrick, 'The corporate governance lessons from the financial crisis'; Peter Yeoh, 'Causes of the global financial crisis: Learning from the competing insights' (2010) 7 International journal of disclosure and governance 42; Gleb Fetisov, 'Measures to Overcome the Global Crisis and Establish a Stable Financial and Economic System: (Proposals for the G-20 on Financial Markets and the International Economy)' (2009) 52 Problems of Economic Transition 20

2.1 Definition of Corporate Governance

Corporate Governance is not a universally understood or agreed upon concept and the broader concept generally includes the responsibility towards stakeholders and shareholders. Corporate Governance, in its broadest sense, refers to a variety of legal and non-legal ideas and practices influencing control of publicly owned commercial enterprises.[8] The European Union created Corporate Governance Codes,[9] which were then updated by the Sarbanes-Oxley Act in 2002[10] before being published by the Organization for Economic Cooperation and Development (OECD), which developed the OECD Principles of Corporate Governance[11] that addressed the globalization of corporate governance and encouraged the responsibility for truthful and ethical reporting in corporate practice.

The Organization for Economic Co-operation and Development (OECD) offers the widely recognized definition of corporate governance, which is acknowledged by most nations and international institutions like the World Bank and the United Nations. The definition of corporate governance in this context is "the system by which business corporations are directed and controlled. The corporate governance structure specifies the distribution of rights and responsibilities among different participants in the corporation, namely, board of directors, shareholders and other stakeholders and spells out the rules and procedures for making decisions on corporate affairs."[12]

---

[8] J Robert Brown and Lisa L Casey, 'Corporate governance: cases and materials' (2012) CORPORATE GOVERNANCE: CASES AND MATERIALS, J Robert Brown, Jr & Lisa L Casey, eds, LexisNexis 11
[9] G Dallas and D Pitt-Watson, 'Corporate governance policy in the European Union' (2016) Through an Investor's Lens (CFA Institute, Hrsg)
[10] Paul Sarbanes, *Sarbanes-oxley act of 2002* (2002)
[11] OCDE OECD, 'The OECD principles of corporate governance' (2004) Contaduría y Administración
[12] Ibid

2.2   The Role of Corporate Governance

Corporate governance, in Shleifer's words,[13] "deals with the ways in which suppliers of finance to corporations assure themselves of getting a return on their investment." The partnership between shareholders and management is defined by corporate governance.[14] It is a reaction to the agency issues brought on by the division of ownership and power. Corporate governance now refers to all the guidelines and restrictions placed on corporate decision-making. According to Wells,[15] effective corporate governance enables a balance between managers' and shareholders' desires.

In order for there to be good corporate governance, shareholders must be adequately informed about the actions of management and managers must have the right incentives to work for them. Adam Smith was the first to articulate the creation of the corporation, according to Dragomir's summary of the historical developments in corporate governance.[16] After that, Berle and Means introduced the current corporate governance theory in 1932,[17] and Jensen and Meckling introduced the agency theory a decade later, in 1976.[18] The Organization for Economic Cooperation and Development established Corporate Governance Guidelines[19] that address the globalization of corporate governance and promote the need for truthful and transparent reporting.

---

[13] Andrei Shleifer and Robert W Vishny, 'A survey of corporate governance' (1997) 52 The journal of finance 737

[14] Hussein Tarraf, 'The role of corporate governance in the events leading up to the global financial crisis: Analysis of aggressive risk-taking' (2011) 5 Global journal of business research 93

[15] H Wells, 'The Birth of Corporate Governance. 33 (4)' (2010) 28 Seattle University Law Review, Retrieved June 2015

[16] Voicu D Dragomir, 'Highlights for a history of corporate governance' (2008) European journal of management

[17] Adolf Augustus Berle and Gardiner Gardiner Coit Means, *The modern corporation and private property* (Transaction publishers 1991)

[18] Michael C Jensen and William H Meckling, 'Theory of the firm: Managerial behavior, agency costs and ownership structure' (1976) 3 Journal of financial economics 305

[19] OECD, 'The OECD principles of corporate governance'

2.3   The 2008 Global Financial Crisis

Clarke correctly pointed out that the Global Financial catastrophe of 2008 was a catastrophe that was genuinely global in scope and that it had an impact on all continents and nations.[20] The fact that the financial crisis of 2008 took place despite the recent improvement in corporate governance in the United States is noteworthy, according to Cheffins.[21] The peak of the stock market in 2000, when the Federal Reserve and the Central Bank of the United States expected a small recession and lowered federal fund rates, was cited by Poole in 2010 as the root cause of this catastrophe.[22] As a result, many mortgages were issued to people with bad credit records.[23] cheap or no down payments and cheap borrowing rates were made available to these borrowers. The three primary causes of the financial crisis, according to Lang and Jagtani,[24] were the phenomenal growth of residential Mortgage-Backed Securities, whose market performance was closely correlated with the continued increase in housing prices; the enormous expansion of the housing market; and the widespread lowering of mortgage underwriting standards.

According to a 2009 report by the Organization for Economic Cooperation and Development's (OECD) Steering Group on Corporate Governance,[25] the financial crisis was caused by flaws and deficiencies in the corporate governance structure. Similar findings were made by the

---

[20] Clarke, 'Recurring crises in Anglo-American corporate governance'
[21] Cheffins, 'Did Corporate Governance" Fail" During the 2008 Stock Market Meltdown? The Case of the S&P 500'
[22] William Poole, 'Causes and Consequences of the Financial Crisis of 2007-2009' (2010) 33 Harv JL & Pub Pol'y 421
[23] Brian Duignan, 'Financial crisis of 2007–08' (2019) 7 Encyclopedia Britannica, October
[24] Lang and Jagtiani, 'The mortgage and financial crises: The role of credit risk management and corporate governance'
[25] Kirkpatrick, 'The corporate governance lessons from the financial crisis'

Shareholder Bill of Rights Act of 2009,[26] which was sponsored by the U.S. Senate. In addition to highlighting regulatory flaws at the national and international levels, United Nations Conference on Trade Development (UNCTAD)'s research of the causes of the 2008 Global Financial Crisis also highlights inadequate corporate governance practices as they are related to the risk management practices followed by many major financial institutions.[27]

A major contributing factor to the financial and economic crisis in the United States, according to the National Commission on the Causes of the Financial and Economic Crisis in 2011,[28] was the "dramatic failure of corporate governance... at many systematically important financial institutions." It is concluded that poor corporate governance was one of the main reasons for the financial and economic problems that plagued the country. Kirkpatrick claimed, more specifically, that the control that businesses need to support ethical business practices and to protect against excessive risk-taking are not provided by corporate governance frameworks.[29]

2.4   Corporate Governance Before the 2008 Global Financial Crisis

There were several noteworthy traits and trends in corporate governance that were pervasive in many nations and businesses prior to the 2008 Global Financial Crisis. In general, the corporate governance environment prior to the 2008 financial crisis showed flaws in risk management, board independence, executive remuneration, and regulatory monitoring. These flaws fueled a culture of reckless risk-taking and lax accountability, which eventually influenced the beginning and scope of the catastrophe.

---

[26] David Tomaselli, 'The Shareholder Bill of Rights: Major Reform or Minor Adjustment' (2011) 13 Duq Bus LJ 59

[27] UNCTAD, *Corporate Governance in the Wake of the Financial Crisis* (United Nations Publication 2010)

[28] US Congress—The Financial Crisis Inquiry Commission, 'The Financial Crisis Inquiry Report: Final Report of the National Commission on the Causes of the Financial and Economic Crisis in the United States' (2011) 30 Washington, DC: US Government Printing Office Accessed May 2016

[29] Kirkpatrick, 'The corporate governance lessons from the financial crisis'

2.4.1 Shareholder Value

The philosophy that dominated corporate governance placed a strong emphasis on maximizing shareholder value and many businesses set out to increase shareholder wealth and provide quick financial returns as their main goals. This emphasis on shareholder profit often resulted in overconfidence and a disregard for the interests of other stakeholders, including staff members, clients, and the larger community.

2.4.2 Risk Management

It is noted that although risk management systems were in place, they often fell short of being successful in identifying and controlling complex risks brought on by financial innovations and the interconnection of the global financial system. The efficacy of risk management procedures was hampered by the usage of complicated financial instruments and poor risk models.

2.4.3 Executive Remuneration

It is noteworthy that remuneration systems for executives were often designed to reward short-term financial success, typically based on indicators like stock price and quarterly profitability. Executives were therefore encouraged as a result to prioritize short-term rewards over risk management or long-term sustainability. The interests of other stakeholders and executive incentives were therefore not in line with one another.

2.4.4 Board Independence

The company's board of directors traditionally included both executive and non-executive directors. The efficacy and independence of non-executive directors were a source of worry as there were instances when non-executive directors' links with the firm or its management lasted for a long time, raising concerns about their capacity to conduct impartial supervision.

2.4.5   Regulatory Frameworks

The laws and rules of conduct in effect for various corporate governance frameworks in different countries varied with inadequate efficacy of regulatory enforcement and monitoring. Due to accelerated financial innovation and the growing complexity of the financial markets, regulatory agencies failed to keep up and there were instances when regulatory flaws and inconsistencies allowed for excessive risk-taking and poor oversight.

2.5   Failures and Weaknesses in the Corporate Governance Arrangements

According to Kirkpatrick,[30] the system had a few flaws that were inherently flawed. The failure of risk management systems was ascribed to poor corporate governance procedures in several of the failing institutions. The risk considerations were not taken into account by the boards of collapsed banks while approving the business plan. In several banks, there was plainly a lack of company disclosures on the predictable risk factors and regarding mechanisms for monitoring and managing risk. Even worse, the accounting and regulatory framework was ineffective. Once again, according to Kirkpatrick,[31] the company's pay systems were not in line with its risk tolerance, strategy, or long-term viability. Dowd established a connection between the corporate accountability and governance failure and the financial management strategy used.[32] The executive compensation schemes are connected to the second reasons of failure listed by Dowd in relation to corporate responsibility and governance.

---

[30] Ibid
[31] Ibid
[32] Kevin Dowd, 'Moral hazard and the financial crisis' (2009) 29 Cato J 141

3.0   LIMITATIONS OF THE STUDY

The corporate governance systems that were shown to have flaws and shortcomings that may be linked to the Global Financial Crisis of 2008 are the exclusive focus of this research essay. The essay is not focused on additional factors that may have contributed to the crisis that are directly related to macroeconomic factors; rather, it is focused on the weakness and failure of corporate governance, which is an oversight function of the company's directors and managers, in preventing financial firms from taking excessive risks.

The essay takes the approach that the breakdown of corporate governance was seen as a fundamental contributor to the 2008 Global Financial Crisis. This failure happened as a consequence of the great majority of the impacted financial organizations' incapacity to stop their directors from making business-risky actions. There are also additional intricate and interconnected factors that contributed to the crisis, including as the US housing bubble, the absence of regulation in the subprime sector, mortgage securitization and banks' exposure to its risk,[33] other than corporate governance that is primary focus of this essay.

4.0   A CRITICAL DISCUSSION OF GRANT KIRKPATRICK'S STATEMENT

While the failures and weaknesses in corporate governance arrangements as contended by Grant Kirkpatrick's statement did contribute significantly to the 2008 Global Financial Crisis, it is important to view them within the broader context of other systemic factors and shared responsibilities. The 2008 Global Financial Crisis revealed deficiencies in risk management, board oversight, executive compensation, transparency, and accountability. This section provides a critical analysis of Grant Kirkpatrick's statement from two divergent perspectives.

---

[33] Grosse, 'The global financial crisis–a behavioral view'

4.1 Merits of Grant Kirkpatrick's Statement

Grant Kirkpatrick's statement, on the one hand, is merited in terms of attributing the 2008 Global Financial Crisis predominantly to the failures and weaknesses in corporate governance arrangements as discussed below:

4.1.1 Poor Risk Management

It is noted that effective risk management is a crucial component of corporate governance. Numerous financial firms' poor risk management procedures were made clear by the 2008 Global Financial Crisis. Despite having access to complicated financial instruments and lending practices, the corporate board of directors and executives failed to effectively examine and comprehend the dangers involved. They over-relied on defective models and under-estimated the systemic risks that could have existed. This served to demonstrate that risk management and evaluation by corporate governance were not done correctly.

4.1.2 Absence of Board Oversight

Corporate governance systems depend on boards of directors to offer oversight and question the choices of the company's management. However, it is observed that several boards lacked knowledge, independence, and active involvement throughout the financial crisis. In other words, they fell short in challenging management tactics, risk tolerance, and general corporate decisions. A lack of corporate governance to provide sufficient board supervision was evident in certain instances when the entire board of directors were not fully aware of the scope of the risks the institutions were incurring.

4.1.3 Lack of Transparency and Accountability

It should be appreciated that to guarantee appropriate operation and reduce risks, corporate governance depends on transparency and accountability. However, the 2008 Global Financial

Crisis brought to light serious shortcomings in the fields of transparency and accountability. Financial firms employed difficult-to-understand, complicated financial instruments, and pertinent information regarding their hazards was often hidden. The disclosure of risk exposures lacked transparency, and there was little or no responsibility for bad choices and actions of the company's management. The efficacy of corporate governance processes was therefore hampered by these shortcomings in accountability and transparency.

4.1.4 Executive Remuneration System

The 2008 Global Financial Crisis made it clear that many financial organizations' executive remuneration systems incentivized taking excessive risks. It was observed that short-term gains were often recognized in executive remuneration packages without proper consideration of long-term risks for the company. Due to the mismatch of incentives, a culture of putting short-term profits above ethical and sustainable business practices developed and the financial crisis was made worse by corporate governance's inability to address these incentive systems, which were meant to deter taking excessive risks.

4.2 Demerits of Grant Kirkpatrick's Statement

On the other hand, Grant Kirkpatrick's statement can be challenged as being too narrow in scope in terms of the viewpoint that maintains that while the 2008 Global Financial Crisis was caused by a number of deficiencies in the procedures and rules regulating corporate governance, other causes also played a significant role in contributing to the crisis as follows:

4.2.1 Failures in Regulation

The 2008 Global Financial Crisis revealed loopholes in the enforcement and regulatory structures of countries. The financial crisis was exacerbated by insufficient oversight, weak or ineffective rules, and regulatory capture. It is critical to recognize that the interaction between regulatory shortcomings and poor corporate governance contributed to the crisis as a whole.

4.2.2 Shared Responsibility

It is observed that although corporate governance was supposed to prevent excessive risk-taking, the crisis cannot be entirely blamed on corporate governance mistakes. Other players included financiers, rating services, auditors, regulators, and decision-makers. The collective failure of many actors and systems should also be taken into account in a thorough evaluation of the aspects that contributed to the financial crisis.

4.2.3 Broader Systemic Causes

While deficiencies in corporate governance had a substantial impact, it is crucial to understand that the 2008 Global Financial Crisis was a complicated event driven by a number of broader systemic causes, which included macroeconomic inequalities, insufficient regulatory monitoring, failures of rating agencies, and excessive risk-taking across the financial sector. It is noted that if these larger structural problems are not taken into account, the financial crisis may be primarily attributed to poor corporate governance, which is entirely not the case.

5.0 CONCLUSION

This essay has critically analyzed and concurs with Grant Kirkpatrick's statement that the 2008 Global Financial Crisis can be to an important extent attributed to failures and weaknesses in corporate governance arrangements. It is observed that according to corporate governance policies, boards must have a thorough understanding of the company's strategy and risk tolerance as well as effective reporting mechanisms that enable quick responses. Monitoring the success of the company's risk management methods and implementing adjustments as necessary would satisfy the board's clear oversight responsibility for risk management.

The essay therefore contends that in an effective corporate governance system, the managers who oversee the day-to-day operations of the company are given sufficient incentives to work for and on behalf of the shareholders, that they have the right incentives to do so, and that information about the managers' activities is properly communicated to the shareholders.

In conclusion, the corporate governance idea has long been founded on the establishment of a board of directors acting on behalf of the shareholders to monitor and guide the administration of the organization. According to this view, a company's performance is primarily determined by its ability to generate a profit and a satisfactory return on investment for its shareholders.[34]

While achieving sustainable economic growth and increasing shareholder equity are the primary goals of strong corporate governance, it is contended that it is also necessary to serve the interests of all stakeholders by ensuring the effective implementation of adequate internal and external controls over the company's operations.

---

[34] Frank Aquila, 'Corporate governance: Don't rush reform' (2009) 9 Business Week

BIBLIOGRAPHY

Berle AA and Means GGC, *The modern corporation and private property* (Transaction publishers 1991)

Laeven ML and others, *Lessons and policy implications from the global financial crisis* (International Monetary Fund 2010)

Sarbanes P, *Sarbanes-oxley act of 2002* (2002)

UNCTAD, *Corporate Governance in the Wake of the Financial Crisis* (United Nations Publication 2010)

Aquila F, 'Corporate governance: Don't rush reform' (2009) 9 Business Week

Blundell-Wignall A, Atkinson P and Lee SH, 'The current financial crisis: Causes and policy issues' (2009) 2008 OECD Journal: Financial market trends 1

Brown JR and Casey LL, 'Corporate governance: cases and materials' (2012) CORPORATE GOVERNANCE: CASES AND MATERIALS, J Robert Brown, Jr & Lisa L Casey, eds, LexisNexis 11

Cheffins BR, 'Did Corporate Governance" Fail" During the 2008 Stock Market Meltdown? The Case of the S&P 500' (2009) The Business Lawyer 1

Clarke T, 'Recurring crises in Anglo-American corporate governance' (2010) 29 Contributions to Political Economy 9

Commission UCTFCI, 'The Financial Crisis Inquiry Report: Final Report of the National Commission on the Causes of the Financial and Economic Crisis in the United States' (2011) 30 Washington, DC: US Government Printing Office Accessed May 2016

Dallas G and Pitt-Watson D, 'Corporate governance policy in the European Union' (2016) Through an Investor's Lens (CFA Institute, Hrsg)

Dowd K, 'Moral hazard and the financial crisis' (2009) 29 Cato J 141

Dragomir VD, 'Highlights for a history of corporate governance' (2008) European journal of management

Duignan B, 'Financial crisis of 2007–08' (2019) 7 Encyclopedia Britannica, October

Fetisov G, 'Measures to Overcome the Global Crisis and Establish a Stable Financial and Economic System: (Proposals for the G-20 on Financial Markets and the International Economy)' (2009) 52 Problems of Economic Transition 20

Grosse RE, 'The global financial crisis–a behavioral view' (2010) Available at SSRN 1537744

Jensen MC and Meckling WH, 'Theory of the firm: Managerial behavior, agency costs and ownership structure' (1976) 3 Journal of financial economics 305

Kirkpatrick G, 'The corporate governance lessons from the financial crisis' (2009) 2009 OECD Journal: Financial market trends 61

Lang WW and Jagtiani JA, 'The mortgage and financial crises: The role of credit risk management and corporate governance' (2010) 38 Atlantic Economic Journal 295

OECD O, 'The OECD principles of corporate governance' (2004) Contaduría y Administración

Poole W, 'Causes and Consequences of the Financial Crisis of 2007-2009' (2010) 33 Harv JL & Pub Pol'y 421

Shleifer A and Vishny RW, 'A survey of corporate governance' (1997) 52 The journal of finance 737

Tarraf H, 'Literature review on corporate governance and the recent financial crisis' (2010) Available at SSRN 1731044

Tarraf H, 'The role of corporate governance in the events leading up to the global financial crisis: Analysis of aggressive risk-taking' (2011) 5 Global journal of business research 93

Tomaselli D, 'The Shareholder Bill of Rights: Major Reform or Minor Adjustment' (2011) 13 Duq Bus LJ 59

Wells H, 'The Birth of Corporate Governance. 33 (4)' (2010) 28 Seattle University Law Review, Retrieved June 2015

Yeoh P, 'Causes of the global financial crisis: Learning from the competing insights' (2010) 7 International journal of disclosure and governance 42